TWELVE IRON PARADOXES

TWELVE IRON PARADOXES

A System of Contradiction

by J. A. Gucci

Instructor Edition

CONTENTS

This collection was developed to complement the formal principles established in Absolute Composition. Rather than operating as philosophical riddles or abstract logical exercises, these poems present observable systems organized through clear structural relationships. They invite close analytical attention to the mechanics of contradiction, persistence, and equilibrium.

To facilitate classroom integration, each instructor note offers four distinct analytical entry points: Paradox Context, System Correspondence, Absolute Composition, and Discussion. Together, these quadrants connect the poem's observable subject matter directly to its compositional architecture, ensuring that classroom analysis remains grounded in verifiable physical processes.

The accompanying discussion questions serve as frameworks for close observation rather than mechanisms for driving toward a single, predetermined interpretation. They offer students a clear methodology for examining how a poem is constructed, how its central triad organizes contradiction, and how structural coherence is maintained despite opposing conditions.

While these poems maintain their structural integrity when read independently, instructors utilizing the Absolute Composition framework will find that its core principles actively inform the entire collection. The notes intentionally employ a shared terminology across both volumes to ensure a fluid, cohesive experience in the classroom seminar environment. Ultimately, this guide functions not to resolve the paradoxes presented by the poems, but to illuminate the structural frameworks through which they remain coherent.

HOW TO USE THIS BOOK

This volume is organized around the dynamics of contradiction rather than the mechanics of interpretation. Each text presents an observable system governed by a three-part structural relationship, or triad. The analytical objective here is not to resolve apparent inconsistencies, but to recognize how physical systems sustain opposing conditions while remaining structurally coherent.

The text suggests reading each poem prior to consulting the accompanying instructor notes. This sequence allows the reader to engage with the poem's immediate paradox before anchoring those observations in the underlying physical context, structural correspondences, and specific compositional mechanisms.

The discussion questions are structured to facilitate close observation rather than open-ended interpretation. By directing analytical attention toward structural relationships, these prompts offer a framework for examining how contradiction is generated, maintained, and ultimately understood through deliberate arrangement.

Readers familiar with Absolute Composition will recognize many of its foundational principles at work across these paradoxes.

Those new to the framework may simply approach these texts as formal studies in contradiction.

Ultimately, these systems do not ask, "How can this be true?" They ask a much more practical question: "How does this system hold?"

*"The system holds.
Contradiction is not an error."*

Paradox I: Identity
Triad: Self / Division / Identity

Paradox Context
An anchor chain secures a vessel by hanging in a suspended
catenary curve between the bow and the sea floor. As slack
accumulates on the bottom, the chain ceases to function as a
suspended curve and collapses into a heap. Once heaped, the
links become susceptible to kinking.

System Correspondence
Self denotes the chain as a continuous object. Division denotes
the structural collapse from suspended curve to heaped slack.
Identity persists because the chain remains the same object
despite its altered configuration.

Absolute Composition
This poem employs **Structural Correspondence.** The chain
remains the governing structure throughout the composition
while its physical configuration changes. The omitted collapse
compresses the transformation, allowing identity to persist
through observable relation rather than explanation.

Discussion
1. How does the chain remain the same object despite changing
its physical configuration?

2. Why does the poem omit the collapse rather than describe it
directly?

3. In what ways does the kink arise from the chain's altered
arrangement rather than from a change in identity?

Paradox I: Identity

Black iron chain
sagging

heap
slumped in silt—

kinked.

Paradox II: Stillness
Triad: Stillness / Division / Identity

Paradox Context

A vibrating string produces a musical pitch determined by its
length, tension, and mass. As the string is wound, its tension
increases, raising the frequency at which it vibrates. Although
its sound changes, the string remains the same physical object
throughout the transformation.

System Correspondence

Stillness denotes the string as a continuous physical object.
Division denotes the transition between the two musical
pitches produced by changing tension. Identity persists
because the string itself remains unchanged while its behavior
is altered.

Absolute Composition

This poem employs **Conceptual Compression.** The process of
tightening the string is reduced to the threshold, "wound—",
allowing the transformation from one pitch to another to
emerge through observable correspondence rather than
mechanical explanation. Identity is preserved while behavior
changes.

Discussion

1. What changes when the string is wound, and what remains
the same?

2. Why does the poem identify the musical notes rather than
describing the physical frequencies?

3. How does the threshold, "wound—", transform the string's
behavior without changing its identity?

Paradox II: Stillness

Still steel
string

SOL,
wound—

LA.

Paradox III: Knowing
Triad: Knowing / Doubt / Knowing

Paradox Context
A rapidly spinning top may appear motionless despite rotating at high speed. Its angular momentum maintains an upright position while slight nutation continually corrects its balance. The appearance of stillness is therefore produced by continuous motion rather than by its absence.

System Correspondence
Knowing denotes the observer's initial assumption that the top is at rest. Doubt emerges as the recognition that the apparent stillness conceals continuous motion. Knowing returns when the observer understands that the top's stability depends upon its rotation rather than contradicting it.

Absolute Composition
This poem employs **Conceptual Compression.** The rotational mechanics that sustain the top are omitted, leaving only the observable relationship between apparent stillness and hidden motion. The threshold remains implicit, allowing the paradox to emerge through structural correspondence rather than explanation.

Discussion
1. Why can a rapidly spinning top appear motionless to an observer?

2. How does the poem move from apparent certainty to doubt and back to understanding?

3. In what ways does omitting the rotational mechanics strengthen the paradox presented by the poem?

Paradox III: Knowing

Sleeping top
nutating—

still.

Paradox IV: Control
Triad: Control / Release / Control

Paradox Context
A drawn bow stores elastic energy as it bends. Upon release,
the arrow flexes rapidly as it passes the bow, correcting its
initial curvature through oscillation while maintaining a stable
trajectory. The apparent instability of both bow and arrow
becomes the condition for accurate flight.

System Correspondence
Control denotes the stored potential within the drawn bow.
Release denotes the transfer of elastic energy from bow to
arrow. Control returns as the oscillating arrow stabilizes in
flight and reaches its intended target.

Absolute Composition
This poem employs **Conceptual Compression.** The instant of
release is omitted, allowing the poem to move directly from
stored energy to observable consequence. By presenting only
the conditions before and after the threshold, the composition
demonstrates how control emerges through the coordinated
behavior of the system rather than through rigid stability.

Discussion
1. Why must both the bow and the arrow bend in order to
produce an accurate shot?

2. How does the omission of the moment of release strengthen
the structural progression of the poem?

3. In what ways does the arrow's oscillation contribute to
control rather than diminish it?

Paradox IV: Control

Bent bow
crooked arrow

still,
oscillating—

bullseye.

Paradox V: Irreversibility
Triad: State / Transformation / Same State

Paradox Context
A coiled steel spring stores elastic energy through deformation.
When compressed and heated beyond its tempering
temperature, the metal's internal structure changes
permanently. After cooling, the spring remains the same object
but can no longer recover its original form or behavior.

System Correspondence
State denotes the spring in its original tempered condition.
Transformation denotes the combined action of compression
and heat that permanently alters the steel's internal structure.
Same State returns as the spring remains recognizably the
same object despite having lost its original elastic properties.

Absolute Composition
This poem employs **Recursive Structural Zeugma.** The spring
governs both the opening and closing states of the
composition, returning as the same physical object while
embodying an irreversible transformation. The correspondence
is preserved not through restored behavior, but through the
persistence of identity across permanent structural change.

Discussion
1. Why is the spring still recognized as the same object after
losing its elasticity?

2. Why must both heat and compression occur together to
produce permanent deformation?

3. How does the poem distinguish between a change in
behavior and a change in identity?

Paradox V: Irreversibility

Cool coiled spring
soft

crushed—
blasted by a blowtorch.

Cool
coiled spring—
rigid.

Paradox VI: Freedom
Triad: Freedom / Constraint / Freedom

Paradox Context
An arch carries weight by directing compressive forces along
its curved structure. As a load is applied, the arch flexes
slightly while maintaining its integrity. When the load is
removed, the structure returns toward its original form
without losing its capacity to bear weight. Temporary
constraint preserves long-term freedom.

System Correspondence
Freedom denotes the arch in its unloaded state. Constraint
denotes the compressive forces temporarily altering its form
beneath a load. Freedom returns as the load is removed and
the arch resumes its original configuration while retaining its
structural function.

Absolute Composition
This poem employs **Recursive Structural Zeugma.** The arch
governs both the opening and closing of the poem, returning to
its initial position after passing through constraint. The
mirrored arrangement of the composition reflects the
observable behavior of the structure itself, allowing recursion
to emerge through formal organization rather than repetition
alone.

Discussion
1. How does the arch support increasing weight without
collapsing?

2. Why does the poem begin and end with the same structural
image?

3. In what ways does temporary constraint preserve, rather
than diminish, the arch's structural freedom?

Paradox VI: Freedom

Arch
flexing

upside-down

flexing
arch.

Paradox VII: Order
Triad: Order / Disruption / Order

Paradox Context
When a container holding particles of different sizes is shaken,
the smaller particles settle through the spaces between the
larger ones while the larger particles rise toward the top.
Known as the Brazil nut effect, this spontaneous reordering
occurs without adding or removing material. Disorder
produces a more organized arrangement.

System Correspondence
Order denotes the initial arrangement of seeds and nuts within
the jar. Disruption denotes the shaking that temporarily
disturbs the system. Order returns as the contents reorganize
into a new, stable configuration determined by particle size
rather than their original positions.

Absolute Composition
This poem employs **Inversion Structural Zeugma**. The
shaking simultaneously governs the reversal of the seeds' and
nuts' positions while preserving the identity of every object in
the system. The composition demonstrates conceptual
compression by presenting only the observable arrangements
before and after disruption, allowing the paradoxical
reordering to emerge through structural correspondence rather
than explanation.

Discussion
1. Why does shaking the jar produce a more organized
arrangement instead of a more random one?

2. What changes in the system, and what remains the same
throughout the poem?

3. How does the inversion of the seeds' and nuts' positions
illustrate the paradox that disruption can generate order?

Paradox VII: Order

Seeds over nuts
settled in a jar

shake—

nuts over seeds
settled in a jar

Paradox VIII: Meaning
Triad: Meaning / Absurdity / Meaning

Paradox Context
Soap bubbles naturally organize into hexagonal patterns as
adjoining films minimize surface energy. When the bubbles
contact a ripe squirting cucumber, the slightest disturbance
triggers the rapid ejection of its seed-bearing fluid. An
apparently orderly structure becomes the initiating condition
for an unexpectedly violent biological response.

System Correspondence
Meaning denotes the orderly hexagonal arrangement of the
soap bubbles. Absurdity denotes the seemingly
disproportionate discharge of the squirting cucumber.
Meaning returns when the observer recognizes that the
explosive response follows directly from the biological
system's stored internal pressure rather than from randomness.

Absolute Composition
This poem employs **Threshold Structural Zeugma**. The point
of contact simultaneously completes the geometric
arrangement of the bubbles and initiates the cucumber's
discharge. A single threshold governs both systems, allowing
the observable correspondence between delicate order and
explosive release to emerge without explanatory narration.

Discussion
1. Why do soap bubbles naturally form hexagonal patterns?

2. How can such a slight disturbance trigger such a rapid
biological response?

3. In what ways does the point of contact function as the
threshold governing both observable systems?

Paradox VIII: Meaning

Soapy hexagons
alight on a pod—

squirting cucumber.

Paradox IX: Cause
Triad: Cause / Effect / Cause

Paradox Context
Water continuously evaporates from Earth's surface, condenses within the atmosphere, and returns as precipitation. A cloudburst appears to terminate the cloud, yet the released water eventually evaporates, condenses, and forms new clouds. The effect of one stage becomes the cause of the next within an uninterrupted hydrologic cycle.

System Correspondence
Cause denotes the developing cloud formed through condensation. Effect denotes the cloudburst that releases accumulated water. Cause returns as the fallen water reenters the hydrologic cycle, giving rise to future clouds and continuing the system.

Absolute Composition
This poem employs **Structural Correspondence**. The observable stages of the water cycle align directly with the governing triad, allowing the conclusion of one event to become the origin of the next. Through conceptual compression, the poem presents only the visible transitions, permitting recurrence to emerge from the continuity of the physical system rather than explanatory narration.

Discussion
1. Why does a cloudburst represent both an ending and a beginning within the water cycle?

2. How does the poem transform an apparent effect into the cause of a future event?

3. In what ways does the recurring behavior of the hydrologic cycle sustain the paradox of continuous causation?

Paradox IX: Cause

Furling cloud
burst

furling.

Paradox X: Presence
Triad: Presence / Absence / Presence

Paradox Context
As a vessel moves through water, it displaces the surrounding
surface, generating a turbulent wake. After the vessel has
passed, the water gradually becomes calm while a lingering
trail of sea foam continues to mark its former path. The source
disappears, yet evidence of its passage remains visible.

System Correspondence
Presence denotes the moving vessel actively disturbing the
water. Absence denotes the vessel after it has departed from
view. Presence returns as the remaining sea-foam trail
preserves the observable effects of what is no longer physically
present.

Absolute Composition
This poem employs **Residual Structure**. The vessel itself is
absent from the composition, leaving only the observable
consequence of its movement. The poem compresses the
transition from active disturbance to lingering evidence,
allowing presence to persist through structural residue rather
than continued occupation.

Discussion
1. Why does the sea-foam trail remain after the vessel has
disappeared?

2. How does the poem distinguish between physical presence
and observable evidence?

3. In what ways does the remaining wake preserve the passage
of something that is no longer there?

Paradox X: Presence

Churched
churning channel

calm—

sea-foam trail.

Paradox XI: Truth
Triad: Truth / Contradiction / Truth

Paradox Context
Although polished glass appears perfectly smooth, every
surface contains microscopic irregularities. When two
exceptionally flat pieces of glass are pressed together, these
irregularities interact through intermolecular forces, causing
the surfaces to adhere. What appears most slippery can
therefore become unexpectedly difficult to separate.

System Correspondence
Truth denotes the observer's recognition that glass is smooth
and slippery. Contradiction denotes the unexpected adhesion
that occurs when two polished surfaces meet. Truth returns as
the apparent contradiction is understood to arise from the
physical behavior of the material itself rather than from an
exception to it.

Absolute Composition
This poem employs **Conceptual Compression.** The
microscopic interactions responsible for adhesion are omitted,
leaving only the observable conditions before and after contact.
The composition preserves the contradiction while allowing
the underlying physical truth to emerge through structural
correspondence rather than explanation.

Discussion
1. Why can two smooth pieces of glass become difficult to
separate?

2. How does the poem distinguish between visual appearance
and physical behavior?

3. In what ways does the omitted microscopic process
strengthen the paradox presented by the poem?

Paradox XI: Truth

Slippery glass
brittle

slippery glass

clutched.

Paradox XII: Being
Triad: Being / Non-being / Being

Paradox Context
A square and a circle each exist as complete geometric forms governed by distinct definitions. When the two are combined into a single object—a square circle—the resulting expression remains grammatically meaningful while becoming geometrically impossible. The language exists; the object cannot.

System Correspondence
Being denotes the independent existence of the square and the circle as valid geometric forms. Non-being denotes the impossible object created by their combination. Being returns as the individual forms retain their logical integrity despite the failure of their composite to exist.

Absolute Composition
This poem employs **Structural Correspondence**. The composition juxtaposes two valid forms whose combination produces an impossible object without altering the integrity of either constituent. By presenting only the observable linguistic arrangement, the poem demonstrates conceptual compression, allowing the paradox to emerge through the correspondence between language and geometry rather than philosophical exposition.

Discussion
1. Why can a square and a circle each exist independently but not as a single object?

2. How does the poem distinguish between the existence of language and the existence of physical form?

3. In what ways does the impossible compound reveal the boundary between conceptual possibility and geometric reality?

Paradox XII: Being

A square
circle

square.

APPENDIX A: PARADOXICAL PHENOMENA AND OBSERVATIONAL FRAMEWORKS

The following terms identify the principal observable phenomena and structural relationships examined throughout *Twelve Iron Paradoxes*. They provide instructors with concise reference points for discussing how contradiction emerges through physical systems rather than abstract speculation.

Cause — The initiating condition within a continuous system from which subsequent observable behavior emerges. See Paradox IX.

Constraint — A force or condition that limits, redirects, or temporarily alters the behavior of a system while preserving its structural integrity. See Paradox VI.

Contradiction — The simultaneous presence of opposing observable conditions that remain physically coherent within the same system. See Paradox XI.

Control — The maintenance of directed behavior through the coordinated interaction of opposing forces rather than through rigidity alone. See Paradox IV.

Division — The structural separation or reconfiguration of a continuous object or system while preserving its identity. See Paradoxes I and II.

Freedom — The capacity of a system to return to equilibrium after passing through temporary constraint. See Paradox VI.

Identity — The persistence of an object's structural continuity despite observable changes in configuration or behavior. See Paradoxes I and II.

Irreversibility — A permanent transformation through which a system retains its identity while losing the capacity to return to an earlier state. See Paradox V.

Order — A stable arrangement that emerges through the interaction or reorganization of a physical system rather than through external imposition. See Paradox VII.

Presence — The observable existence of a system, whether through direct occupation or through the residual evidence of its effects. See Paradox X.

Stillness — An apparent state of rest that may arise from continuous motion or equilibrium within a dynamic system. See Paradox III.

Truth — The observable behavior of a system as determined by its physical structure rather than by initial appearance or expectation. See Paradox XI.

APPENDIX B: COMPOSITIONAL FRAMEWORKS AND STRUCTURAL MECHANISMS

The following compositional mechanisms appear throughout Twelve Iron Paradoxes. Each represents a practical application of the broader principles developed in **Absolute Composition**. The descriptions below are intentionally concise and serve as reference points for classroom discussion rather than complete theoretical treatments.

Structural Correspondence — The formal alignment between the observable behavior of a physical system and the governing triadic structure of the composition.

Threshold Behavior — The observable transformation that occurs when a system passes through a critical point of change while preserving its structural continuity.

Threshold Structural Zeugma — A variation of structural zeugma in which the governing element occupies the precise point of systemic transformation, concentrating the threshold into a single observable condition.

Inversion Structural Zeugma — A structural zeugma in which the governing element organizes an observable reversal of orientation, relation, or structural order.

Recursive Structural Zeugma — A structural zeugma in which the governing element returns the system to its point of origin while preserving evidence of transformation.

Structural Compression — The synthesis of multiple physical or chronological transitions into a single continuous textual sequence.

Conceptual Compression — The omission of explanatory mechanisms while preserving the observable structural transformation they produce.

Residual Structure — A compositional arrangement that presents the remaining evidence of a completed process after the originating force has withdrawn.

For comprehensive theoretical development, extended examples, and the complete taxonomy of compositional mechanisms, instructors are encouraged to consult Absolute Composition.

APPENDIX C: TRIAD TAXONOMY AND SYSTEM MAPPING

The following index maps the three-part structural relationships, or triads, that govern each paradox's compositional architecture. Each triad organizes the progression of observable conditions and structural contradictions presented throughout the volume.

Paradox I: Identity
Self / Division / Identity

Paradox II: Stillness
Stillness / Division / Identity

Paradox III: Knowing
Knowing / Doubt / Knowing

Paradox IV: Control
Control / Release / Control

Paradox V: Irreversibility
State / Transformation / Same State

Paradox VI: Freedom
Freedom / Constraint / Freedom

Paradox VII: Order
Order / Disruption / Order

Paradox VIII: Meaning
Meaning / Absurdity / Meaning

Paradox IX: Cause
Cause / Effect / Cause

Paradox X: Presence
Presence / Absence / Presence

Paradox XI: Truth
Truth / Contradiction / Truth

Paradox XII: Being
Being / Non-being / Being

GLOSSARY OF CENTRAL TERMS

Absolute Composition — A formalist methodology in which poetic structure is modeled directly on observable physical systems, structural correspondences, and transformation dynamics, prioritizing objective relationships over symbolic interpretation.

Contradiction — The coexistence of opposing observable conditions within a single system while maintaining structural coherence.

Observation — The analytical practice of identifying and following the structural behavior of a physical system before assigning conceptual or thematic interpretation.

Persistence — The capacity of a system to retain its identity or governing behavior despite undergoing transformation, opposition, or disruption.

Structural Correspondence — The formal alignment between the observable behavior of a physical system and the compositional architecture that models it.

System — An organized arrangement of interacting elements whose observable relationships generate stable behavior, transformation, or contradiction within defined conditions.

Threshold Behavior — The observable
transformation that occurs when a system passes
through a critical point of change while preserving
its underlying structural continuity.

Triad — The foundational three-part relational
architecture used to organize each paradox within
this volume, mapping a progression from an initial
condition, through an opposing force, to a
structurally coherent outcome.

Note: For comprehensive theoretical expansions,
axiomatic proofs, and extended pedagogical
histories of these mechanisms, instructors are
encouraged to consult the foundational volume,
Absolute Composition.

THE TWELVE SERIES

Each book in this series presents systems through short, structured poems.

Rather than describing events, the poems model how systems form, interact, and change over time.

Each volume focuses on a different civilization, using the same method to reveal how complex societies develop.

History

Twelve Clay Tablets (Mesopotamia)
Twelve Desert Floods (Egypt)
Twelve Marble Questions (Greece)
Twelve Roman Thresholds (Rome)
Twelve Medieval Thresholds (Medieval World)

Creative Writing

Twelve Small Windows
Twelve Loops
Twelve Mirrors
Twelve Rooms

Philosophy

Twelve Iron Paradoxes

ABOUT THE AUTHOR

J. A. Gucci is a writer, educator, and independent theorist whose work explores the relationship between poetic form, observable systems, and structural composition. He is the originator of **Absolute Composition**, a formalist methodology that models literary structure on the behavior of physical systems rather than symbolic interpretation.

His research integrates insights from optics, mechanics, thermodynamics, hydrology, biology, and cognitive perception to develop practical frameworks for reading and writing poetry. Through both creative and theoretical works, he advocates for a systems-based approach to composition in which meaning emerges from structural correspondence rather than metaphorical substitution.

He is the author of **Absolute Composition** and the Twelve series.

COLOPHON

Twelve Iron Paradoxes: A System of Contradiction was composed in Palatino, an exceptionally legible serif typeface designed by Hermann Zapf in 1948 and modeled after the geometry of Italian Renaissance calligraphy.

The body text is set at 9-point type on a uniform 5.5 by 8.5 inch page layout. The typographic arrangement was engineered to balance structural compression with visual clarity, reflecting the formal compositional dynamics detailed throughout the text.

Designed, produced, and issued by Pressure System Press. Manufactured and printed in the United States of America.

www.ingramcontent.com/pod-product-compliance
Lightning Source LLC
Chambersburg PA
CBHW021347060726
47591CB00006B/2207